CHANGED THROUGH FAITH ACTION PLAN

30-DAY ACTIVATION GUIDE

CW01496558

BRIAN GOSLEE

Changed Through Faith Action Plan
© 2019 by Brian Goslee.

All rights reserved. Printed in the United States of America.

Published by Author Academy Elite
P.O. Box 43, Powell, OH 43065
www.AuthorAcademyElite.com

Softcover: 978-1-64085-706-3
E-book: 978-1-64085-708-7

Available in softcover and e-book.

CONTENTS

_____'s

CHANGED THROUGH FAITH ACTION PLAN

Welcome! Write your name in the blank. As you write your name, accept God's love for you and believe it. This is important because God cares about you—*personally and by name*. Your name matters, your life matters, and you are special to God. As you prayerfully work your way through this plan, God will provide peace and guidance that are *especially for you*.

This is *your* plan to grow in your faith and relationship with God and to activate change in your life. To experience change in your life, you have to do things differently. As you apply this plan, you will discover new peace, purpose, and joy through a daily, active faith in God.

HOW TO USE THIS PLAN

This action plan is designed to be completed consistently for one month, followed by one month of accountability and journaling as you continue to live a life changed through faith. Each step of the plan is designed to take one week. Daily readings and activation steps will guide your journey. Here are some tips to maximize your experience:

> ➢ Use the checkboxes to guide your activity and track your progress.
> ➢ Read the weekly reminders out loud.
> ➢ Don't go through this alone—connect with others one-on-one or in a small group.
> ➢ Discuss your answers on items marked with a speech icon.

The *Changed Through Faith Action Plan* is not intended as a stand-alone book; it is a resource for the CTFaith small groups (in-person and virtual), coaching programs, and online courses. It is important to share with others and be in community as you go through this if possible. These programs are available at ctfaith.com and will help you activate the life change and faith development steps in the book *Changed Through Faith: Four Steps to Activating a Life of Peace, Purpose, and Fulfillment.*

CHANGED THROUGH FAITH

Set your mind on things above and pursue
God with active faith through the four steps.

Believe. Receive. Live It. Give It.

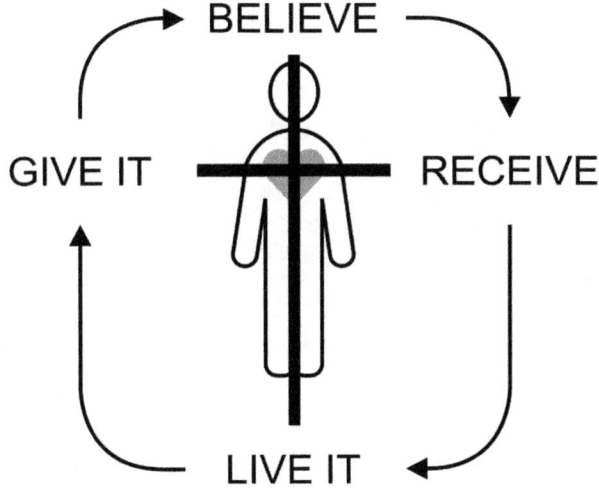

GOALS

What do you want to get out of this experience? List one to three goals for your growth and development as you implement your Changed Through Faith Action Plan.

ACTIVATE YOUR FAITH
STEP 1: BELIEVE

When you believe, you make a decision. God doesn't want you to leave your brain out of the journey of faith. He wants you to use your mind as you follow Him. He wants to help you think more like Him. Believe and trust in who God is and decide daily to put Him first in your life through a relationship with Jesus Christ.

BELIEVE STATEMENT

Read this out loud every day this week.

> I BELIEVE God is who He says He is, has a great plan for me, and delivers on His promises. It doesn't mean I don't ever have doubt, but the boldness of my belief helps me forge ahead despite any doubt or fear.

DAY 1

BELIEVE THROUGH THE BIBLE

Read the daily Bible passage and write your reflections about it. Take note how the readings are helping you

> ➢ Believe in God.
> ➢ Believe in God's view of you, instead of believing negative self-talk.
> ➢ Believe in what God and the Bible say about your situation.

For I am sure that neither death nor life, nor angels nor rulers, nor things present nor things to come, nor powers, nor height nor depth, nor anything else in all creation, will be able to separate us from the love of God in Christ Jesus our Lord. (Romans 8:38-39 ESV)

☐ How can this help you BELIEVE?

Engaging consistently with God's Word in the Bible is a vital part of building your relationship and belief in God. Your faith and trust are strengthened as you learn God's promises and how He has demonstrated His faithfulness and love.

☐ How can reading the Bible daily move you toward your goals from page 5?

DAY 2

And without faith it is impossible to please him, for whoever would draw near to God must believe that he exists and that he rewards those who seek him. (Hebrews 11:1 NLT)

☐ How can this help you BELIEVE?

BELIEVE THROUGH PRAYER

☐ What do you believe about God? What do you struggle to believe about God? What do you want to believe about God?

Prayerfully consider your answers above, then write a prayer to God that reflects what you believe about Him and your life and what you need help believing.

Example: Lord, I pray as the man in the Bible story who brought his son to you for healing, "I believe; help my unbelief!" I believe you are the all-powerful, all-knowing, all-loving Creator of the universe and the Lord of my life. Help me walk forth boldly in this belief every day. Amen.

☐ Write your prayer below and pray it.

DAY 3

Everyone who believes that Jesus is the Christ has become a child of God. And everyone who loves the Father loves his children, too. We know we love God's children if we love God and obey his commandments. Loving God means keeping his commandments, and his commandments are not burdensome. For every child of God defeats this evil world, and we achieve this victory through our faith. And who can win this battle against the world? Only those who believe that Jesus is the Son of God. (1 John 5: 1-5 NLT)

☐ How can this help you BELIEVE?

BELIEVE THROUGH RELATIONSHIPS

Reflect on your current relationships. Check any steps you currently take and work toward a new one. You don't have to do everything at once, but you will experience growth as you move through them all.

☐ I have told someone about my journey through this plan and my desire to grow and activate my faith in God.

☐ I meet regularly with a person in my life who is a genuine Christian whom I consider to be more mature in their spiritual journey.

☐ I am active in a Christian-based or Bible-based small group (in person or online) that meets regularly.

☐ I meet regularly with a person in my life who I help with their faith development or personal growth.

The first step in activating your faith through relationships is to intentionally build them. In some relationships, especially early in your spiritual growth journey, you are more often the learner. In other relationships, you are more often the teacher or mentor. The key is to do this action plan with others—not alone. If you are not in these types of relationships, visit ctfaith.com and learn how you can join online small groups and coaching programs.

DAY 4

It was by faith that Abraham obeyed when God called him to leave home and go to another land that God would give him as his inheritance. He went without knowing where he was going. (Hebrews 11:8 NLT)

☐ How can this help you BELIEVE?

BELIEVE THROUGH A RENEWED MIND

➢ Believe the promises of God instead of the lies of culture and the enemy.
➢ Live by faith in God instead of fear in your situation.
➢ Know that you are not alone.
➢ Realize that your faith development, like your life, is a journey of many seasons.
➢ Wherever you are right now is just *one season*, not the whole picture.

☐ Write down one or two circumstances that are challenging you in this season/time of your life:

1.

2.

For each situation you wrote down, read and pray the prayers below and <u>replace your fear with belief</u> in what these prayers say about your circumstance.

☐ (Prayer based on Romans 8:28)
God, I <u>believe</u> by faith that You make all things work together for my good. I love You and I am loved and chosen to be part of Your plan. I know that You are with me in this circumstance and it will be used to Your glory, even when I can't see how. I <u>believe</u> this in faith.

☐ (Prayer based on John 20)
God, I <u>believe</u> in Your provision, healing, and caring for me in this situation, no matter what evidence I see with my human eyes. Blessed are those who have not seen and yet <u>believe</u>. By faith, I <u>believe</u> and trust in You. God, please bless me and strengthen me in this faith.

DAY 5

"But you are my witnesses, O Israel!" says the Lord. "You are my servant. You have been chosen to know me, believe in me, and understand that I alone am God. There is no other God—there never has been, and there never will be. I, yes I, am the Lord, and there is no other Savior." (Isaiah 43:10-11 NLT)

☐ How can this help you BELIEVE?

ACTIVATE YOUR FAITH

Your focus shapes your thoughts, and your thoughts shape your behavior. An attitude of gratitude makes a big impact on how you approach God and your belief in Him.

☐ Make a list of things for which you are grateful. Display the list and be reminded to give God thanks for these blessings.

✓

✓

✓

✓

Look around you for God's power, influence, and provision. If you look for it, you will see it. Be aware and ready for evidence of God at all times. ***You will find what you look for.***

DAY 6

For God so loved the world that he gave his one and only Son, that whoever believes in him shall not perish but have eternal life. For God did not send his Son into the world to condemn the world, but to save the world through him. (John 3:16-17 NIV)

☐ How can this help you BELIEVE?

STORIES ABOUT BELIEF

☐ Who do you know in real life or in culture who demonstrates strong belief in God?

☐ Look through the stories in Chapter 4 of the *Changed Through Faith* book (Joey, Andrea, father & child in the Gospel of Mark, and Randy). Which one of these do you connect with the most and why?

Describe a *Believe story* that happened in your life and imagine a *Believe story* that could happen for you in the future using these writing prompts:

☐ *I demonstrated strong belief in God when I …*

☐ *I will demonstrate strong belief in God in the future by …*

DAY 7

"I am praying not only for these disciples but also for all who will ever believe in me through their message. I pray that they will all be one, just as you and I are one—as you are in me, Father, and I am in you. And may they be in us so that the world will believe you sent me." [Jesus prayer to the Father] (John 17: 20-21 NLT)

☐ How can this help you BELIEVE?

ACTIVATE PEACE THROUGH BELIEVING

Through this week's action steps, you have built *belief* in who God is and who you are because of your relationship with Him.

☐ Write down how this *belief* has created, or will create, more peace in your life.

If you are not experiencing more peace yet, don't worry, you will. You will look at this more in the next step: *Receive*. Write down potential obstacles to experiencing an increase in peace. Remember, (a) it's only been a week, and (b) if you are continuing some bad habits or habitual sin, that may be blocking your peace.

☐ Congratulations! You've completed the BELIEVE step of your action plan. How have you moved one step closer to your goals from page 5?

ACTIVATE YOUR FAITH
STEP 2: RECEIVE

You should be intentional about receiving from God. This keeps you in position to live out your faith consistently and experience a life of greater peace and purpose. A car only runs when it has gasoline in it, so we make it a point to go to a gas station and put fuel in it. Likewise, you need to spend time with God and take intentional steps to fill up with the fuel for life that He has for you.

RECEIVE STATEMENT

Read this out loud every day this week.

> As I believe in faith, I expect and pray to RECEIVE God in my heart and life, and all that He offers me — His power, plans, and provision. It is one thing to believe, but I now take the next step to RECEIVE from Him. This is an important part of my relationship and experience with God. I will proceed in faith. I will have patience and be consistent, and I will remember... it takes time.

NOTE: If you have never started a personal relationship with God through Jesus Christ and you want to do that, please reach out to a member of our team now. Tell them you are on Step 2 of the *CTFaith Action Plan* and want to start a relationship with Jesus and accept Him as Lord and Savior of your life. Visit ctfaith.com for contact information.

DAY 1

BELIEVE THROUGH THE BIBLE

Read the daily Bible passage and write your reflections about it.

Take note how the reading is helping you

> ➤ Receive God's love, forgiveness, and peace.
> ➤ Receive how God values you, instead of believing negative self-talk.
> ➤ Receive increased understanding about yourself or a situation in your life.

But to all who did receive him, who believed in his name, he gave the right to become children of God. (John 1:12 ESV)

☐ How can this help you RECEIVE?

LISTENING PRAYER STEPS AFTER READING

This week, after you read your Bible passage, spend the allotted amount of time in silence. Listen for God to prompt you or speak to you in some way. You may be drawn to a meaning of a certain word or phrase. You might be prompted to some action or application. Every two days check off the time and increase to the next level.

☐ one minute
☐ two minutes
☐ three minutes

☐ Write down thoughts, revelations, or action items from your listening prayer time.

DAY 2

I pray that from his glorious, unlimited resources he will empower you with inner strength through his Spirit. Then Christ will make his home in your hearts as you trust in him. Your roots will grow down into God's love and keep you strong. And may you have the power to understand, as all God's people should, how wide, how long, how high, and how deep his love is. May you experience the love of Christ, though it is too great to understand fully. Then you will be made complete with all the fullness of life and power that comes from God. (Ephesians 3:16-19 NLT)

☐ How can this help you RECEIVE?

RECEIVE THROUGH PRAYER

☐ What do you need to receive from God right now regarding your current circumstances? What prayer request do you have related to your spiritual growth (e.g., forgiveness, love, wisdom, etc.)?

Prayerfully consider your answers above, then write a prayer to God below and pray.

Example: Lord, let Your wisdom take over in place of my thinking.
Let Your Spirit of faith and boldness replace my spirit of fear and insecurity.
Help me put my trust and hope in You. I surrender all I have and all I am into Your hands. Amen.

☐ Write your prayer and pray it.

DAY 3

Do not be conformed to this world, but be transformed by the renewal of your mind, that by testing you may discern what is the will of God, what is good and acceptable and perfect. (Romans 12:2 ESV)

☐ How can this help you RECEIVE?

RECEIVE THROUGH RELATIONSHIPS

Reflect on your current relationships. Check any steps that you currently take and work toward a new one. You don't have to do everything at once, but you will experience growth as you move through them all.

☐ I have told someone about my journey through this plan and my desire to grow and activate my faith in God.

☐ I meet regularly with a person in my life who is a genuine Christian whom I consider to be more mature in their spiritual journey.

☐ I am active in a Christian-based or Bible-based small group (in person or online) that meets regularly.

☐ I meet regularly with a person in my life who I help with their faith development or personal growth.

☐ List the name of one person who helps you live a life that's changed through faith because you *Receive* from them.

☐ Pray to receive from God the name of a person who you will help to live a life that's changed through faith because *they will receive from you*. If someone comes to mind, write their name and pray for them frequently. You will list this person again in the GIVE IT section.

DAY 4

God showed how much he loved us by sending his one and only Son into the world so that we might have eternal life through him. This is real love—not that we loved God, but that he loved us and sent his Son as a sacrifice to take away our sins. (1 John 4:9-10 ESV)

☐ How can this help you RECEIVE?

RECEIVE THROUGH A RENEWED MIND

Make room to *receive* from God.

☐ What drives you each day?

☐ What is the first thing you need to unclench your grip on to make more room to receive from God?

Based on your answers above, think about a change you can make that will put "following God" as the answer to the question, "What drives you?"

☐ One change I need to make that will put <u>following God</u> as the driving force in my life is:

☐ After you write down any changes you think of, share them with your CTFaith group, Quick Check Partner, or close friend. It may take time to accomplish it, but that is okay. Remember, you are likely already making an adjustment as part of this program. Recognize it and write it down. It will be a powerful reminder for you that you're on the right track!

Do you have an area of hurt, hang-up, pain, or addiction that is hard to break or affecting your progress? If so, I encourage you to reach out for help from your church, a family member, friend, or celebraterecovery.com. Know and have confidence that God can crush those areas with His almighty healing power and the power of His Holy Spirit for those who trust in Him and seek true repentance!

DAY 5

"Ask, and it will be given to you; seek, and you will find; knock, and it will be opened to you. For everyone who asks receives, and the one who seeks finds, and to the one who knocks it will be opened." [Jesus speaking] (Matthew 7:7-8 ESV)

☐   How can this help you RECEIVE?

ACTIVATE YOUR FAITH

Read *It's About Love* and think about how you can *receive* from God. Next, respond with two things listed in the poem that you most need to accept and receive from God.

IT'S ABOUT LOVE

by Brian Goslee

God has a plan for my life because He loves me.

God lets me suffer and grow because He loves me.

God encourages me because He loves me.

God speaks to me through others, the Bible, songs, and directly because He loves me.

God wants to spend time with me because He loves me.

God lets me experience discipline because He loves me.

God gave me the freedom to choose because He loves me.

God wants me to be aligned with His Spirit because He loves me.

God allowed His Son to be crucified on a cross because He loves me.

God wants the best for me because He loves me.

☐ What two things mentioned in the poem do you most need to accept and receive from God?

☐ Stop now and pray to God for that. Write down any thoughts or revelations about those items afterward.

DAY 6

And after you have suffered a little while, the God of all grace, who has called you to his eternal glory in Christ, will himself restore, confirm, strengthen, and establish you. To him be the dominion forever and ever. Amen. (1 Peter 5:10-11 ESV)

☐ How can this help you RECEIVE?

STORIES ABOUT RECEIVING FROM GOD

☐ Who do you know in real life or in culture who demonstrates *receiving from God* in a strong way?

☐ Look through the stories in Chapter 5 of *Changed Through Faith* (the healed woman in Matthew 9, Tom, Trevor, and Julie). Which one of these do you connect with the most and why?

Describe a *Receive story* that happened in your life and imagine a *Receive story* that could happen for you in the future using these writing prompts.

☐ *I received from God when I …*

☐ *I will receive from God when I …*

DAY 7

The Lord is compassionate and merciful, slow to get angry and filled with unfailing love. He will not constantly accuse us, nor remain angry forever. He does not punish us for all our sins; he does not deal harshly with us, as we deserve. For his unfailing love toward those who fear him is as great as the height of the heavens above the earth. He has removed our sins as far from us as the east is from the west. (Psalm 103:8-12 NLT)

☐ How can this help you RECEIVE?

ACTIVATE PEACE THROUGH RECEIVING

Through this week's action steps, you have learned to *receive* from God in prayer, through the Bible, and through relationships.

☐ Write down how receiving from God in these ways has created or will create more peace in your life.

☐ Congratulations! You've completed the RECEIVE step of your action plan! How have you moved one step closer to your goals from page 5?

ACTIVATE YOUR FAITH
STEP 3: LIVE IT

You will see a theme in the stories contained in the *Changed Through Faith* book and in the Bible: Until people started living out their faith actively, they didn't experience true transformation and the full impact of living purposeful lives. Live out your faith daily to experience real change in your life and the lives of others. Put your faith into action!

LIVE IT STATEMENT

Read this out loud every day this week.

> With my heart and mind focused on God, I want to live out my faith to experience real change in my own life and affect change in the lives of others. Today, I will put my faith into action and LIVE IT.

DAY 1

LIVE IT THROUGH THE BIBLE

Read the daily Bible passage and write your reflections about it.

Take note how these Bible readings are helping you live out your faith actively.

But don't just listen to God's word. You must do what it says. Otherwise, you are only fooling yourselves. (James 1:22 NLT)

☐   How can this help you LIVE IT?

LISTENING PRAYER STEPS AFTER READING

After you read your Bible passage, spend the allotted amount of time in silence. Listen for God to prompt you or speak to you in some way. Afterward, write down whatever comes to mind. Don't be concerned with whether they are your thoughts or God's thoughts. You only need to write them down. Every few days, check off the time and increase to the next level.

☐   three minutes
☐   four minutes
☐   five minutes

☐   Write down thoughts, revelations, or action items from your listening prayer time.

DAY 2

And now, dear brothers and sisters, one final thing. Fix your thoughts on what is true, and honorable, and right, and pure, and lovely, and admirable. Think about things that are excellent and worthy of praise. Keep putting into practice all you learned and received from me—everything you heard from me and saw me doing. Then the God of peace will be with you. (Philippians 4: 8-9 NLT)

☐ How can this help you LIVE IT?

LIVE IT THROUGH PRAYER

☐ Are there certain places or times in your life where you live out your faith strongly? Are there environments, activities, or relationships in your life that point you in the opposite direction from living out your faith in God?

Prayerfully consider your answers above, then write a prayer to God below and pray.

Example: Lord, I want my relationship with You to be active in my life. Please help me be closer to You as I dedicate more time and trust in You. Help me to avoid tempting situations or activities that take me away from You and Your will for me. Amen.

☐ Write your prayer below and pray it.

DAY 3

Since God chose you to be the holy people he loves, you must clothe yourselves with tenderhearted mercy, kindness, humility, gentleness, and patience. Make allowance for each other's faults, and forgive anyone who offends you. Remember, the Lord forgave you, so you must forgive others. Above all, clothe yourselves with love, which binds us all together in perfect harmony. (Colossians 3:12-14 NLT)

☐ How can this help you LIVE IT?

LIVE IT THROUGH RELATIONSHIPS

Reflect on your current relationships. Check any steps you currently take and work toward a new one (check all that apply).

☐ I have told someone about my journey through this plan and my desire to grow and activate my faith in God.

☐ I meet regularly with a person in my life who is a genuine Christian whom I consider to be more mature in their spiritual journey.

☐ I am active in a Christian-based or Bible-based small group (in person or online) that meets regularly.

☐ I meet regularly with a person in my life who I help with their faith development or personal growth.

☐ Write down an interaction you had that involved LIVING IT this week.

☐ How did your increased awareness to LIVE IT affect the situation?

DAY 4

So you must live as God's obedient children. Don't slip back into your old ways of living to satisfy your own desires. You didn't know any better then. But now you must be holy in everything you do, just as God who chose you is holy. For the Scriptures say, "You must be holy because I am holy." (1 Peter 1:14-16 NLT)

☐ How can this help you LIVE IT?

LIVE IT THROUGH A RENEWED MIND

☐ Print and post this chart as a daily reminder to *Live It*.

LIVE IT CHART

LIVING IT	NOT LIVING IT
Focus is on God	Focus is on me
Faith, not fear	Fear, not faith
God's way	The world's way
Joy	Frustration
Peace	Anxiety
Generosity	Greed
Loving unconditionally	Loving with conditions
Full surrender to God	Partial surrender to God
Gratitude	Wanting what's owed to me
Listening and obeying how God tells me how to live	Asking God to bless the way I want to live

☐ Looking at the chart, identify a way you applied a LIVING IT principle this week instead of a NOT LIVING IT principle and write it down.

☐ Which LIVING IT statement(s) from the chart do you need to focus on?

DAY 5

"Be strong and courageous, for you are the one who will lead these people to possess all the land I swore to their ancestors I would give them. Be strong and very courageous. Be careful to obey all the instructions Moses gave you. Do not deviate from them, turning either to the right or to the left. Then you will be successful in everything you do. Study this Book of Instruction continually. Meditate on it day and night so you will be sure to obey everything written in it. Only then will you prosper and succeed in all you do. This is my command—be strong and courageous! Do not be afraid or discouraged. For the Lord your God is with you wherever you go." [God speaking to Joshua after Moses died] (Joshua 1:6-9 NLT)

☐ How can this help you LIVE IT?

 ## ACTIVATE YOUR FAITH — CHANGE YOUR FILTER

What's in it for me? This is often the filter we use to make decisions. It seems we are not willing to devote our time or money to an activity or purpose unless we sense there is something in it for us.

Instead, try these new filters for the decisions you make. You can apply these to how you spend your time and money, treat others, or motivate yourself.

➤ *What's in it for God?*
➤ *Will this give God glory?*
➤ *Will this bring me and others closer to God?*

Applying these new filters will help you:

> ➤ Activate your faith in God seven days a week.
> ➤ Imitate Jesus and not culture.
> ➤ Love others the way Jesus did.
> ➤ Align with God's will for you.

God loves you. He is for you and not against you. God created you and provides for you. He owns it all, including the blessings and the struggles. When you realize you don't own *anything*, you learn to love and live the way Jesus did.

ACTIVATE YOUR FAITH: *What's in it for Him?*

Think about a decision you must make about an upcoming activity or situation. Apply one of the filters above. Write down the filter you applied and the outcome of how it helped you *live out* your faith.

☐ *The new filter I applied was*:

☐ *The outcome was*:

DAY 6

And do not bring sorrow to God's Holy Spirit by the way you live. Remember, he has identified you as his own, guaranteeing that you will be saved on the day of redemption. Get rid of all bitterness, rage, anger, harsh words, and slander, as well as all types of evil behavior. Instead, be kind to each other, tenderhearted, forgiving one another, just as God through Christ has forgiven you. (Ephesians 4:30-32 NLT)

☐ How can this help you LIVE IT?

STORIES ABOUT LIVING IT

☐ Who do you know in real life or in culture who demonstrates *Living It* in a strong way?

☐ Look through the stories in Chapter 6 in the *Changed Through Faith* book (Brian, Gordon, Lauren, and the apostle Paul). Which one of these resonates with you the most and why?

Describe a *Live It* story that happened in your life and imagine a *Live It* story that could happen for you in the future using these writing prompts:

☐ *I demonstrated living out my faith in God when I...*

☐ *I will demonstrate living out my faith in God by ...*

DAY 7

Rejoice always, pray without ceasing, give thanks in all circumstances; for this is the will of God in Christ Jesus for you. (1 Thessalonians 5:16-18 ESV)

☐ How can this help you LIVE IT?

ACTIVATE PURPOSE & FULFILLMENT THROUGH LIVING IT

☐ *Living it* through these action steps has brought more purpose and fulfillment into my life in the following ways:

☐ Congratulations! You've completed the LIVE IT step of your action plan. How have you moved one step closer to your goals from page 5?

ACTIVATE YOUR FAITH
STEP 4: GIVE IT

Activation of your faith is not only for your benefit, but it is also for the benefit of others. We all need to come to the realization, "It's not about me." As you grow and become *changed through faith*, you will develop a greater capacity to serve others, love them, and help them discover God is active in their lives.

LIVE IT STATEMENT

Read this out loud every day this week.

> I will remember that my faith development is not only
> for my own growth and benefit, but it is also for others.
> Living a life of generosity with my time, talents, treasures,
> compassion, and Christ-like love is what God wants me to do.
> He wants me to GIVE IT away.

DAY 1

GIVE IT THROUGH THE BIBLE

Read the daily Bible passage and write your reflections about it. Take note how these Bible readings are helping you share your faith, give generously, and serve others actively.

Most important of all, continue to show deep love for each other, for love covers a multitude of sins. Cheerfully share your home with those who need a meal or a place to stay. God has given each of you a gift from his great variety of spiritual gifts. Use them well to serve one another. (1 Peter 4:8-10 NLT)

☐   How can this help you GIVE IT?

DAY 2

Remember this: Whoever sows sparingly will also reap sparingly, and whoever sows generously will also reap generously. Each of you should give what you have decided in your heart to give, not reluctantly or under compulsion, for God loves a cheerful giver. (2 Corinthians 9:6-8 NIV)

☐ How can this help you GIVE IT?

GIVE IT THROUGH PRAYER

☐ Is there an area or project where God has been prompting you to give? How can you develop an open-hand, open-heart attitude and act on it?

Prayerfully consider your answers above, then write a prayer to God below and pray it out loud every day this week.

Example: God, help me to see and love others the way that You do. Reveal to me what they need and let me meet their need. Help me learn how You want me to give Your love away and then do it. Amen.

☐ Write your prayer below and pray it.

DAY 3

From the rising of the sun to its setting, the name of the Lord is to be praised! (Psalm 113:3 ESV)

☐ How can this help you GIVE IT?

GIVE IT THROUGH RELATIONSHIPS

You have repeated this step each week and tried to check off all of them. Why? Because you can't love, serve, and teach others when you are by yourself. *To Give It*, you need to be with someone else. When you share your story with someone, mentor them, or pray with them, you love, serve, and teach.

Check any of these steps you currently take:

☐ I have told someone about my journey through this plan and my desire to grow and activate my faith in God.

☐ I meet regularly with a person in my life who is a genuine Christian whom I consider to be more mature in their spiritual journey.

☐ I am active in a Christian-based or Bible-based small group (in person or online) that meets regularly.

☐ I meet regularly with a person in my life who I help with their faith development or personal growth.

☐ How have your relationships changed or grown over these last four weeks?

☐ Have you had any key conversations in which you received support or pro-
vided support regarding faith in God?

DAY 4

Don't just pretend to love others. Really love them. Hate what is wrong. Hold tightly to what is good. Love each other with genuine affection and take delight in honoring each other. Never be lazy but work hard and serve the Lord enthusiastically. Rejoice in our confident hope. Be patient in trouble and keep on praying. When God's people are in need, be ready to help them. Always be eager to practice hospitality. (Romans 12:9-13 NLT)

☐ How can this help you GIVE IT?

GIVE IT THROUGH A RENEWED MIND

You may often believe you don't have anything to give. That's not true. God put something in you. You can give things that are tangible and intangible. He gave you talents, thoughts, time, and treasures of many types. Recalibrate your thoughts through this simple reading and the application that follows:

If your gift is to encourage others, be encouraging. If it is giving, give generously. If God has given you leadership ability, take the responsibility seriously. And if you have a gift for showing kindness to others, do it gladly. Don't just pretend to love others. Really love them. Hate what is wrong. Hold tightly to what is good. Love each other with genuine affection, and take delight in honoring each other. (Romans 12:8-10 NLT)

Spend a few minutes praying and ask God what He wants you to give and then answer the following questions.

☐ What do you have that you can give? (List two things—time, talent, resources, etc.)

☐ How and where will you give it?

DAY 5

Let us hold tightly without wavering to the hope we affirm, for God can be trusted to keep his promise. Let us think of ways to motivate one another to acts of love and good works. And let us not neglect our meeting together, as some people do, but encourage one another, especially now that the day of his return is drawing near. (Hebrews 10:23-25 NLT)

☐ How can this help you GIVE IT?

ACTIVATE YOUR FAITH

In Chapter 7 of *Changed Through Faith*, you learned Jesus *Gave It* in four main ways: loving, serving, teaching, and obeying. Review this at the beginning of Chapter 7.

In this action step, we are focusing on following God's lead. God has things for you to get done. He wants you to give through loving and serving others. It is going to require obedience. Your job is to obey. The result is God's job.

☐ How is God asking you to *follow His lead* in *Giving It*? Write your answer below.

☐ How will you obey God's plans for *Giving It*?

List one person or group you will help (or have helped) by *Giving It* and how you will do that. You may have written down the name of a person in the Receive step under *Day 3*. If so, this is where you put their name.

What will you give? For example, you can share your story, your encouragement, your money, or more (check all that apply).

☐ I will help _____ (name) and GIVE to them through (check all that apply)

   ☐ Serving
   ☐ Loving
   ☐ Forgiving
   ☐ Mentoring
   ☐ Sharing my story of faith
   ☐ Sharing my specific talents
   ☐ Sharing financial resources
   ☐ Praying with them
   ☐ Other (describe)

Afterward, reflect on what happened.

☐ How did the person react/receive it?

☐ Did this experience encourage you to give again, or did it make you hesitant?

If it made you hesitant to *Give It* again the next time, examine if that is a fear you need for God to help you get over, or if it is a healthy learning point that is steering you toward another way of *Giving It*.

DAY 6

Bless those who persecute you. Don't curse them; pray that God will bless them. Be happy with those who are happy, and weep with those who weep. Live in harmony with each other. Don't be too proud to enjoy the company of ordinary people. And don't think you know it all! Never pay back evil with more evil. Do things in such a way that everyone can see you are honorable. Do all that you can to live in peace with everyone. (Romans 12:14-19 NLT)

☐ How can this help you GIVE IT?

STORIES ABOUT GIVING IT

☐ Who do you know in real life or in culture who demonstrates *Giving It* in a strong way?

☐ Look through the stories in Chapter 7 in the *Changed Through Faith* book (Charley, Denny, Nick, Brian, and Peter and John from the book of Acts). Which one of these resonates with you the most and why?

Describe a *Give It story* that happened in your life and imagine a *Give It story* that could happen for you in the future using these writing prompts:

☐ *I demonstrated Giving It when I …*

☐ *I will demonstrate Giving It by …*

DAY 7

For you have been called to live in freedom, my brothers and sisters. But don't use your freedom to satisfy your sinful nature. Instead, use your freedom to serve one another in love. For the whole law can be summed up in this one command: "Love your neighbor as yourself." (Galatians 5:13-14 NLT)

☐ How can this help you GIVE IT?

☐ Congratulations! You've completed the GIVE IT step of your action plan. How have you moved one step closer to your goals from page 5?

ACTIVATE PURPOSE & FULFILLMENT THROUGH GIVING:

☐ *Giving It* through these action steps has brought more purpose and fulfillment in my life in the following ways:

Congratulations! You have finished your *Changed Through Faith Action Plan*. This is a great milestone and we want to celebrate with you! Please email support@ ctfaith.com with FINISHED CTF in the subject line so we can acknowledge your progress and provide encouragement.

Brian Goslee, *Changed Through Faith*

CHANGED THROUGH FAITH
ACTION PLAN JOURNAL

You will experience change in your life if you intentionally apply your action plan. It's easy to fall into the trap of just thinking about God on Sundays, but we need to activate our faith every day.

This journal is meant to take you through your next month after you completed the four-week action plan. However, you can move at your own pace and skip around as you feel led to journal on each topic.

As you take this plan with you and continue to live a life *Changed Through Faith*, it is important to do three things:

1. Have the Word of God immediately available in your mind to keep you moving forward.

2. Have your personal take-aways available to help you *Believe*, *Receive*, *Live It*, and *Give It*.

3. Continue communicating with at least one CTFaith Quick Check Partner or close friend who has been through this with you and understands it.

I hope this journal is a tremendous blessing and catalyst for continued transformation in your life!

Live a life *Changed Through Faith*,

Brian Goslee
Founder, Author, Speaker, & Coach
Changed Through Faith
brian@ctfaith.com

THE CHANGED THROUGH FAITH
QUICK CHECK

This plan is about living a life *Changed Through Faith*. Ask a friend to join you as your CTFaith Quick Check Partner. Every week call each other and check in on these items.

1. BELIEVE
   - ☐ How are you doing with *Believe*?
   - ☐ Are you believing the promises and Word of God or the lies of culture and the enemy?
   - ☐ Are you operating out of fear or faith?

2. RECEIVE
   - ☐ How are you doing with *Receive*?
   - ☐ Did you read the Bible at least three times this week?
   - ☐ Have you listened to God quietly at least three times this week?
   - ☐ Are you reading the Bible passively or actively *receiving* God's love, forgiveness, ideas, and plans?

3. LIVE IT
   - ☐ How did you *Live It* this week?
   - ☐ If people followed you with a news camera, would they see evidence of time spent with God?

4. GIVE IT
   - ☐ Are you *Giving It* away?
   - ☐ Have you given away time or money this week to someone who needed it and to your church?
   - ☐ Did you share a personal story related to your faith this week?
   - ☐ Did you show unconditional love this week?

BELIEVE

My Bible Verses for BELIEVE

Look back at the daily Bible readings from BELIEVE. Write down the book, chapter, and verses of the passage that impacted you the most. Memorize one verse from it.

Book of the Bible _____ Chapter_____ Verse numbers_____

Describe the impact it had on you and your next step related to this.

My Take-Away from BELIEVE

Take some time to read through the completed BELIEVE section from your action plan. After some thought and listening prayer, write down your biggest take-away(s). Here are some questions to help you get started.

- How have I started to experience change in *Believing* God and living that out?
- What do I still need work on with *Believe*?

My Quick Check for BELIEVE

☐ Am I believing the promises and Word of God or the lies of culture and the enemy?

☐ Am I operating out of fear or faith?

Along with the items above, share your *BELIEVE Scripture* and *BELIEVE take-away* with your Quick Check Partner or a close Christian friend. Write down the important points from your conversation.

Other notes and reflections on BELIEVE:

RECEIVE

My Bible Verses for RECEIVE

Look back at the daily Bible readings from RECEIVE. Write down the book, chapter, and verses of the passage that impacted you the most. Memorize one verse from it.

Book of the Bible_____ Chapter_____ Verse numbers_____

Describe the impact it had on you and your next step related to this.

My Take-Away from RECEIVE

Take some time to read through the completed RECEIVE section from your action plan. After some thought and listening prayer, write down your biggest take-away(s). Here are some questions to help you get started.

- How have I started to experience change in *Receiving* from God and living that out?
- What do I still need work on with *Receive*?

My Quick Check for RECEIVE

- ☐ Have I listened to God quietly at least three times this week?
- ☐ Am I reading the Bible passively or actively *Receiving* God's love, forgiveness, ideas, and plans as I read?

Along with the items above, share your RECEIVE Scripture and RECEIVE take-away with your Quick Check Partner or a close Christian friend. Write down the important points from your conversation.

Other notes and reflections on RECEIVE:

LIVE IT

My Scripture for LIVE IT

Look back at the daily Bible readings from LIVE IT. Write down the book, chapter, and verses of the passage that impacted you the most. Memorize one verse from it.

Book of the Bible_____ Chapter_____ Verse numbers_____

Describe the impact it had on you and your next step related to this.

My Take-Away from LIVE IT

Take some time to read through the completed LIVE IT section from your action plan. After some thought and listening prayer, write down your reflections. Here are some questions to consider:

- How have I started to experience changes in *Living It*?
- What do I still need work on related to *Living It*?

My Quick Check for LIVE IT

- ☐ Am I living out my faith consistently?
- ☐ If people followed me with a camera, would they see evidence that I spent time with God?

Along with the items above, share your LIVE IT Scripture and LIVE IT take-away with your quick check partner or a close Christian friend. Write down the important points from your conversation.

Other notes and reflections on LIVING IT:

GIVE IT

My Scripture for GIVE IT

Look back at the daily Bible readings from GIVE IT. Write down the book, chapter, and verses of the passage that impacted you the most. Memorize one verse from it.

Book of the Bible_____ Chapter_____ Verse numbers_____

Describe the impact it had on you and your next step related to this.

My Take-Away from GIVE IT

Take some time to read through the completed GIVE IT section from your action plan. After some thought and listening prayer, write down your reflections. Here are some questions to consider:

- How have I started to experience changes in *Giving It*?
- What do I still need work on related to *Giving It*?

My Quick Check for GIVE IT

- ☐ Have I had any faith-based conversations?
- ☐ Have I given away time or money this week to someone who needed it or to my church?
- ☐ Did I share a personal story related to my faith this week?
- ☐ Did I forgive someone this week or ask for forgiveness?
- ☐ Did I show unconditional love this week?

Along with the items above, share your GIVE IT Scripture and GIVE IT take-away with your quick check partner or a close Christian friend. Write down the important points from your conversation.

Other notes and reflections on GIVING IT:

ABOUT THE AUTHOR

Brian Goslee is an author, speaker, teacher and faith development coach. He is the founder of Changed Through Faith Ministries, a nonprofit organization that helps fathers and families grow closer to God and each other. Brian has been married to Andrea for 27 years and they have two great children, Jordan and Lauren. Brian is active as an author and guest speaker. You can contact him at brian@ctfaith.com and learn more at CTFaith.com.